Diary of a Monarch Butterfly

Library of Congress Catalog number: 75-1793
Trade ISBN: 8027-6267-0
Printed in the United States of America

Text Copyright © 1976 by Susan L. Thompson
Graphics Copyright © 1976 by Sas Colby
Detail Drawings Copyright © 1976 by Judy LaMotte

Distribution by
WALKER AND COMPANY
720 Fifth Avenue
New York, N.Y. 10019

Diary of a Monarch Butterfly

by Susan L. Thompson

Graphic Design by Sas Colby
with detail drawings by Judy LaMotte

MagiCircle PRESS

July 7

Sara and I went hunting for insects this morning.
It was so hot we lay down in the grass.

1

Suddenly a field cricket jumped on a milkweed.
The tall plant moved back and forth.
We lazily watched it sway under the cricket's weight.

2

Then I spotted tiny dots on the underside of the leaves.
"Eggs!" I shouted. "Let's bring them in and watch them."

We broke off a shoot of the plant and carried it to the house.

Carefully we placed it in a large glass jar where the eggs would be safe.

Sara got out her hand lens and we discovered the eggs were those laid by the female Monarch butterfly. The eggs are tiny, pointed, and creamy white, with many small ridges. There seems to be a small spot of black in each egg.

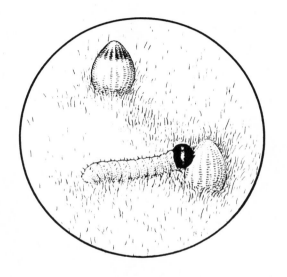

July 8

Just before lunch, I noticed that one caterpillar was beginning to eat his way through the top of its egg.

The second caterpillar came out around 4:00 p.m. Now I know the black spots I saw in the eggs yesterday are the heads of the caterpillars.

Sara and I agreed to take turns putting fresh
milkweed stalks in the jar each day for our friends.

July 10

Today is my turn to change the leaves in the jar. Since the caterpillars are so small, I use a paintbrush to pick them up. When they are safely on the brush bristles, I clean out the bottle and put in a fresh milkweed stalk.

10

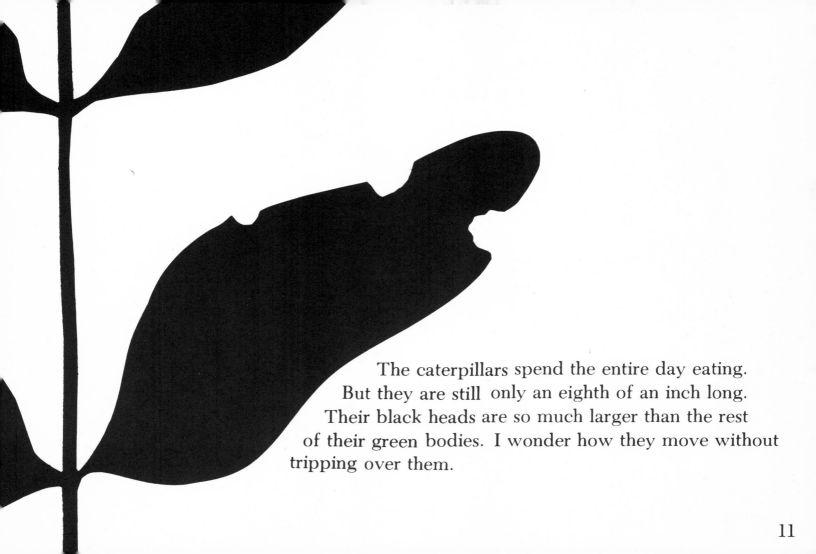

The caterpillars spend the entire day eating.
But they are still only an eighth of an inch long.
Their black heads are so much larger than the rest
of their green bodies. I wonder how they move without
tripping over them.

July 12

Sara discovered that one of the caterpillars had died this morning.

I found a small spider on one of the leaves and think it may be to blame.

Now that the spider is outside the jar, our remaining caterpillar should be safe. It eats and eats and eats, unaware of any dangers.

13

July 19

I watched the caterpillar shed its skin for the third time today, and our new caterpillar is beautiful. The yellow, black, and white stripes on its back are becoming wider and easier to see. Two black feelers have grown behind its head. Two shorter ones poke out from its hind end. It is about one inch long. Sara says it grew too fat and long for its old skin so it left it for a new one.

July 20

We almost lost our caterpillar this morning. When we discovered it was not in the jar, we began looking around the jar.

Suddenly, Sara spied it under her bed, almost 5 feet from its home!

We put it back in the jar, on a milkweed leaf, and set off to make a tinfoil top for its home. With a pencil, we poked many holes in the tinfoil so it would have enough fresh air.

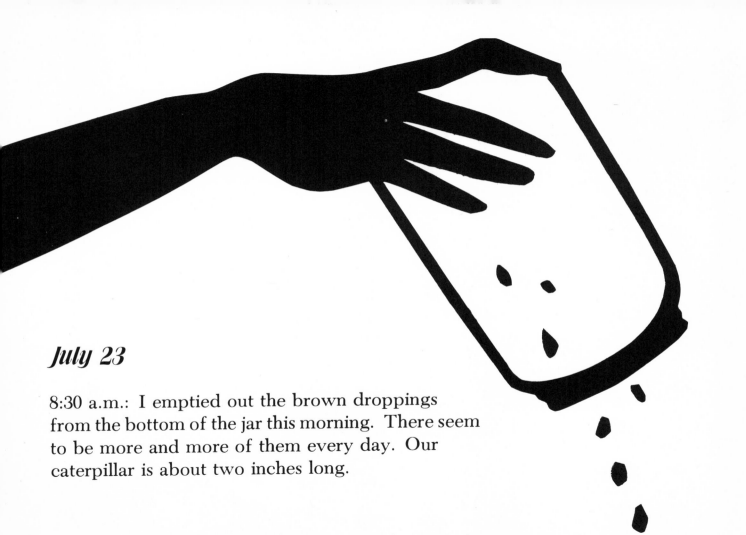

July 23

8:30 a.m.: I emptied out the brown droppings from the bottom of the jar this morning. There seem to be more and more of them every day. Our caterpillar is about two inches long.

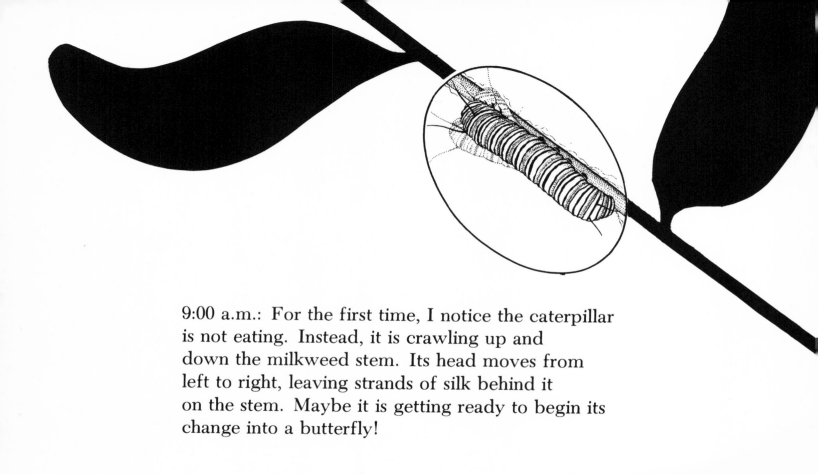

9:00 a.m.: For the first time, I notice the caterpillar is not eating. Instead, it is crawling up and down the milkweed stem. Its head moves from left to right, leaving strands of silk behind it on the stem. Maybe it is getting ready to begin its change into a butterfly!

20

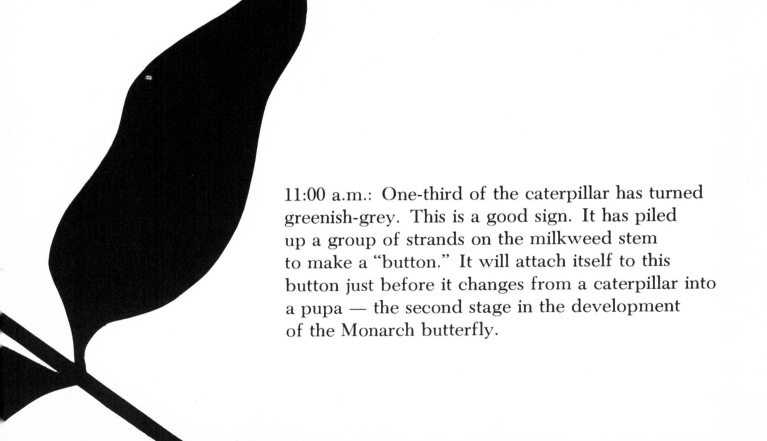

11:00 a.m.: One-third of the caterpillar has turned greenish-grey. This is a good sign. It has piled up a group of strands on the milkweed stem to make a "button." It will attach itself to this button just before it changes from a caterpillar into a pupa — the second stage in the development of the Monarch butterfly.

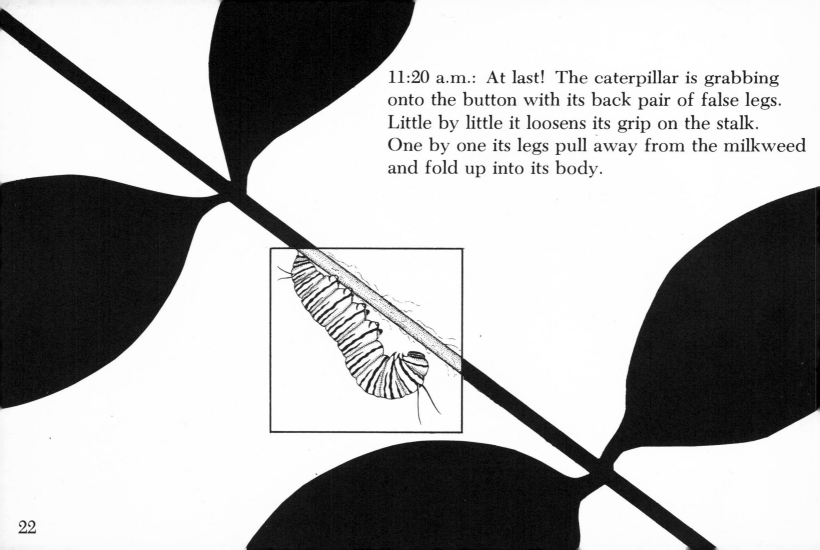

11:20 a.m.: At last! The caterpillar is grabbing onto the button with its back pair of false legs. Little by little it loosens its grip on the stalk. One by one its legs pull away from the milkweed and fold up into its body.

22

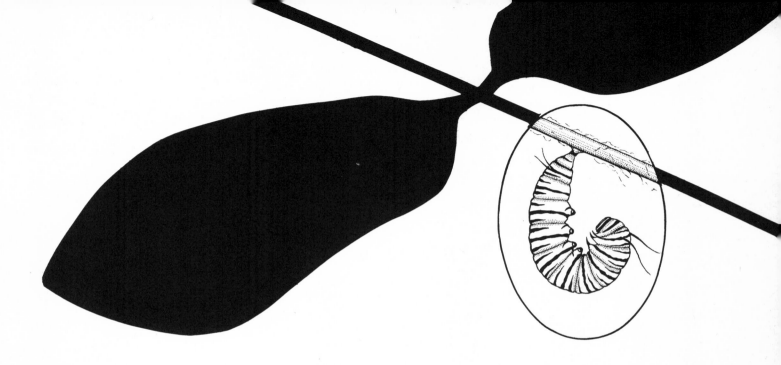

1:00 p.m.: Just before lunch, the caterpillar took
its legs, one pair at a time, off the stalk.
Now all its legs are free and it is hanging from
the white silk button, in the shape of the letter "J."

23

Sara and I ate our lunch in the bedroom. We did not want to disturb the caterpillar by bringing the jar into the kitchen. The smallest movement of the jar sends it swinging. Sara and I agreed we would be especially careful not to hit the jar accidentally.

25

8:00 p.m.: Before bed. I don't want to go to sleep
tonight. Our caterpillar is changing so often that
I'm afraid it will turn into a pupa without us.
But Mom and Dad have promised to check the jar
every hour before they go to bed.

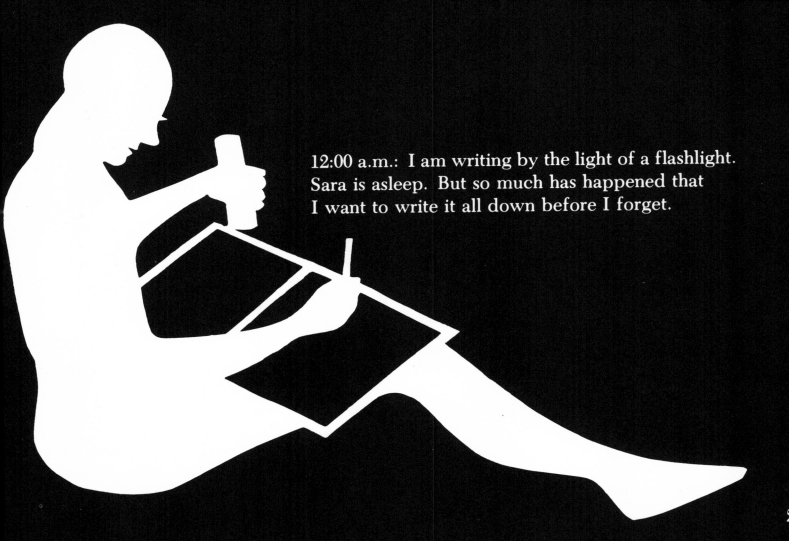

12:00 a.m.: I am writing by the light of a flashlight. Sara is asleep. But so much has happened that I want to write it all down before I forget.

27

Mom and Dad woke me at 11:00 tonight. They saw the caterpillar suddenly begin twisting and turning from its button. When I got up, the skin at the front of the caterpillar had begun to split open.

For a few minutes it worked, pulling itself toward the button. Its body seemed to get fatter and shorter each time it moved. Finally, it shed its entire skin. It fell to the bottom of the jar in a black heap. What was once our caterpillar is now a green form. This green form, the pupa, hangs from the silk button. There are no legs, no feelers, and no body segments in this pupa.

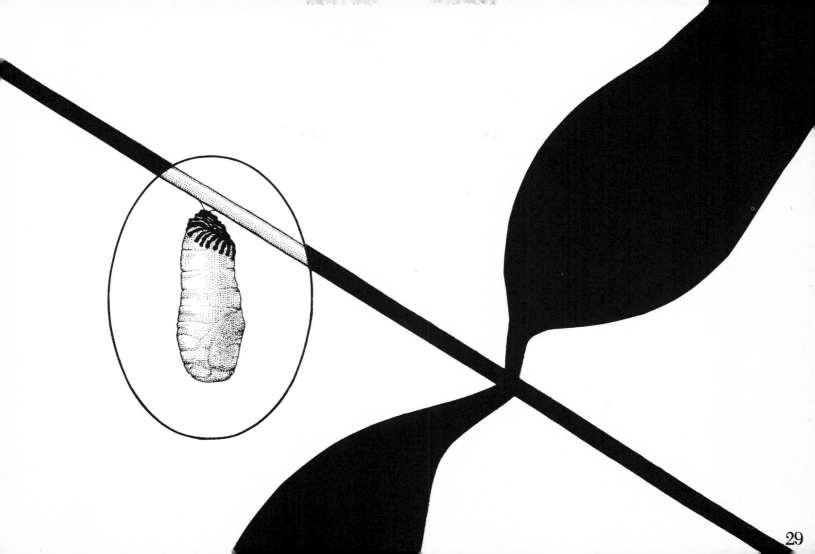

29

July 24

I slept late today. When I woke, our green pupa had
changed its shape slightly. I'm sorry I missed
this. Sara and I went to the library and took some
books out on butterflies. We read that the Monarch
pupa is often called "the green house with the
golden nails," for small gold spots cover the green
form.

When we got back, Sara held a light bulb
behind the jar and the light shone evenly through
the green pupa. The organs of the caterpillar
had disappeared completely!

31

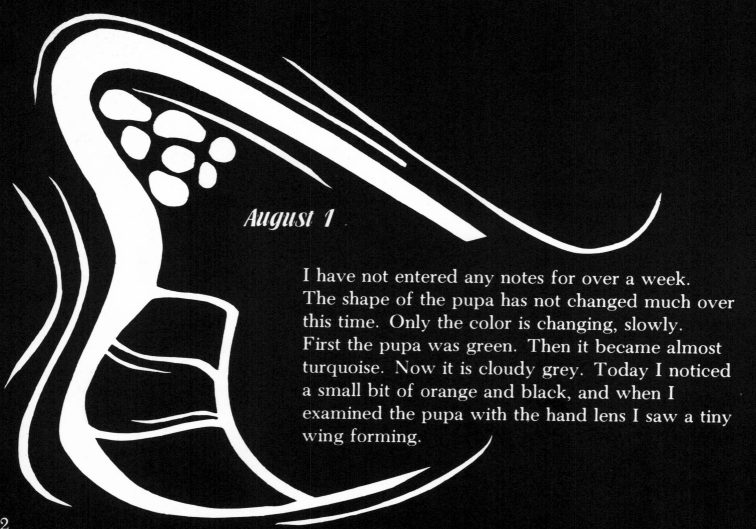

August 1

I have not entered any notes for over a week.
The shape of the pupa has not changed much over
this time. Only the color is changing, slowly.
First the pupa was green. Then it became almost
turquoise. Now it is cloudy grey. Today I noticed
a small bit of orange and black, and when I
examined the pupa with the hand lens I saw a tiny
wing forming.

August 2

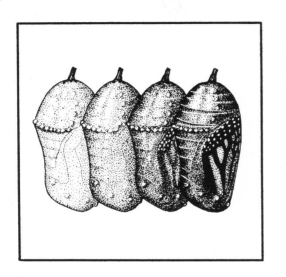

10:00 a.m.: The warm morning sun has turned our pupa almost black. The tiny wings are more clear now. It can't be long before the butterfly will burst out of its shell. I keep a watch over it every minute.

2:00 p.m.: Where do I begin? One hour after
I wrote in the journal this morning, a bright-colored
black, white, and orange Monarch butterfly burst
the walls of its pupa. It hung from the clear
shell with its long, black legs. Slowly it pumped
the liquid from its fat body into its wrinkled
wings. Now and then orange-brown liquid would
drop to the bottom of the jar. This whole
process took about one hour.

When Sara saw that the wings of the butterfly were hardening, we carefully took the jar outside. I put my finger next to the butterfly and it quickly walked onto it. It rested there for a long time.

I wondered if the Monarch was already tame or if it was too tired to be afraid of me.

Gently, I passed the Monarch to Sara. She put it on a milkweed flower and we watched it open its wings slowly, once and then again. For the first time, we saw the Monarch was a male — two large dots marked his lower wings.

At first, when the Monarch used his wings, they carried him only in skips and jumps over the grass. He rested and would begin again.

Finally, he tried and up, up he went, flapping his wings
again and again, skimming over purple milkweed flowers, and
Queen Anne's Lace, up into the wind — happy to be alive, happy to have wings!

Sara and I stayed
until our Monarch disappeared over the horizon,
hoping that perhaps next year he would return, this time with a mate
to lay her eggs on a milkweed leaf in our meadow.

NEW MAGIC CIRCLE PRESS BOOKS

Little Boat Lighter Than a Cork
    by Ruth Krauss and Esther Gilman

Stars In My Sky (Maria Montessori, Anais Nin, Frances Steloff)
    by Valerie Harms

Voices From Within: The Poetry of Women in Prison

Waste of Timelessness and Other Early Stories
    by Anais Nin